101 Things Every Blogger Must Know

By Ekene Onuorah

Copyright Page

This book is a product of research work from the author and has not been copied from elsewhere. It is presented to you as a guide and not to be shared in any form elsewhere, unless with permission from the author.

To contact the author, please email ekeneonuorah@gmail.com

First Published 2016

(C) Ekene Onuorah 2016
ISBN: 978-1-329-88408-3

Revised 2019

Dedication

This work is dedicated to all the bloggers of this world. It contains secrets I've learnt over time - those secrets and tips some bloggers may not like to share. But here are those secrets in plain writings. Take only the tips you need and recommend the book to others – that's why it is dedicated to you.

About the Book

Coming directly from an author who has acquired years of experience in blogging, website designing, programming, online marketing and media advertising, this book provides very helpful tips to both new and established bloggers. The 101 Tips are not to be joked with, and the secrets revealed in here aren't something one can get anywhere on the internet, except in this book. It covers the issues experienced with starting a new blog, choosing a niche, generating ideas, creating content, driving traffic to market the content, getting an Adsense account, monetizing a blog with Google Adsense and other similar programs, maintaining traffic, increasing a blog's worth, making lots of money with a blog and what not.

Preface

Felix was seriously typing, the keyboard producing continuous boring clicks that sounded like our generator. If you've experienced epileptic power supply and lived in a neighborhood where everyone owns a generator, you will know how annoying that sound could be. Although I was distracted from the movie I was watching, I tried to prove to him that I was stronger and could focus. But he won after about five minutes.

"When did you learn to type that fast?" I asked him, but I was talking to myself.

Felix did not flinch a bit. He instead bent closer to my computer and continued typing. He wore an eyeglass I would probably call 'Google' even though it's a Goggle. I was pushed to confront him for fear that he might be doing harm to my computer. There were two things I was sure of: I never typed that fast, and I thought him how to boot a computer.

I approached, thinking that he would stop, but he continued. I looked at the screen and found a window open – a Notepad program. What could he be doing with Notepad? It is just an ordinary text editor, not meant for rich-text formatting. I drew closer to look at what he was doing, and was short of words.

"00001110010010010010011100001100001010001..." Space wouldn't let me complete it and he still typed. I assumed he was trying to form a picture with the arrangement of those binary numbers, but it made no sense.

"Felix, what are you doing with those? You're joking with my computer?"

He shook his head and pointed at a magazine next to the laptop he was typing on. I picked it up and read a portion he highlighted with red biro:

"With the way things are evolving, everyone who hopes to succeed in this technological era must have basic understanding of the internet, and must be able to instruct a computer - that's where being nerdy comes in; ultimately, you must have need to CODE."

I stopped there. The highlighted text was longer. "So, you're coding?" I asked him, taking note of a similarity between his 'Google' and that of a cartoon drawn on the page.

He smiled and nodded. "Just trying to be a nerd! Love my glasses? See my code! Wait till I build Facebook!"

It looked like he was joking.

Today, I still try to remind Felix of this funny event, and it makes him laugh. It reminds me of what determination is – to the extent of fooling one's self. Felix was willing to code that he did anything to make it seem like he was coding. He is now a certified programmer, building Africa's most used web programs. Felix made me want to be a nerd too. He inspired me from that day when the keyboard made more noise than our generator.

That piece of article in that magazine was less than 500 words, but more than 5000 persons were positively changed with its words. It was so prophetic that even now, everyone, almost anyone who read it would always want to end up as a nerd.

This same thing is happening in the field of blogging. Almost everyone wants to be a blogger. This led me into research and to come up with these **101 Things Every Blogger Must Know.**

1. You must have a niche

Welcome to the world of blogging. Every blog must have a niche and your niche has a lot to do with how successful you are going to be in your new field. A niche is like a specialized category, topic or field your blog talks about. Think about a market where only vehicle parts are sold – that's their niche. Think about another market where only sporting equipments are sold – that's another niche.

Now let us put niche in perspective. If you love football, then I'm sure Goal.com is a place you read sports news all the time. Football is the niche of Goal.com, not even the entire sports. Your niche, depending on how people tend to develop interest in it could span across several categories or just within a category or just a single sub-category.

Blogs like ESPN and Super Sports handle everything sports. But Goal.com post only about football which is a sub-category of sports.

Your Niche must be about something you love, something you know a lot about, something you are willing to research about, something you can learn more about, and something you think people would love to follow. Think about Horse races as a niche. But you may end up appealing to only a few. Think about fashion, celebrity gossip and trends as a niche.

Blogs like Mediatakeout.com and TMZ.com have perfected the art of celebrity gossip. But they mostly focus on celebrities in the US and UK. Why not think about your own country? Perez Hilton is also a good example of a celebrity blog. Think about Health, Insurance, Tax matters, movies etc. There are endless niches you can take advantage of today.

Choose a Niche and start working on your blog now.

2. Content is king

So many people go into blogging not knowing what is required of them. As a blogger, you are to create content. What is content then? Content can be anything. It can be an article, it can be a story – a fictional one for that matter, it can be a piece of advice, it can be a picture, and it can be a video.

Content is endless. Even a tweet can end up becoming the content. If you noticed, some authors of the blogs you read can just screen grab or screen capture a tweet, a Facebook post and write about it.

You may be walking on the road and witness an event, take a photo and write about that. A video can also be shot of events and uploaded to become part of the content.

Content is not date of post, author, number of readers/page views etc. Content is usually made up of two things: A title and the content body. The body can be just a picture, write-up, a video or a combination.

One thing to take note of is that your content must always blend to your niche. Write about things your readers care about because they are in your blog because of the niche you have chosen.

To build a good followership, you must post content that blend to the theme and niche.

3. Traffic is queen

Traffic is queen is not an exaggeration. In fact, Traffic should have been the king, but a blog is nothing without the content. Equally, a blog with content is nothing without traffic. The two are at the same level of significance and mutually benefit each other. Traffic and content make a good blog.

What is traffic? Traffic in terms of automobile is the movement of vehicles on a road in a certain area. Think of that area as your blog or website. Then think of the vehicles as people browsing or surfing the internet. This gives us a simple straight-forward definition of traffic.

Traffic is the number of visitors on a certain website, and in our case blog, usually within a specific duration. Yes time matters in traffic. Someone got 1,000,000 visitors to a blog and just broke the news, but before I could scream it was followed up with – in the entire 20 years lifetime of the blog. A blog can get up to 100 visitors in a day, another up to 5000 in a day, another up to 50,000 in a day, but that's not all that matters.

Traffic is also a measure of page views. A visitor can navigate across multiple pages in a blog while another will leave after consuming the content of a page. That's where the term bounce rate comes in. A blog with lower bounce rate and fewer visitors could prove to be better than a blog with huge visitors and an extreme bounce rate, sometimes.

A blog with 500 visitors a day and lower bounce rate could end up having 2000 page views that same day while another with 900 visitors a day with higher bounce rate could end up seeing just 1000 page views.

We will look at how to keep visitors later on.

4. Traffic does not come from no where

Yes, several people believe that people will just find their website automatically as soon as they start publishing great content, without realizing that great content alone is not enough to make one a blogger. Every blogger must be a great marketer too, unless your job is strictly to create content, write or collect information like journalists.

A Journalist may not need to do anything more other than create content, but a blogger must drive traffic to the content created.

There are many sources that traffic could come from, and most of them require that money be spent. This is the headache of most new bloggers. Newbie bloggers want to make money, but wouldn't want to spend. That's why you find many enjoying Google's Blogger and still using .blogspot.com domain. It's not that these new bloggers don't have money for a domain name – they want to make sure they can make money first before they risk spending on a domain name.

Is that the kind of person you will talk to about investing to drive traffic? Traffic does not come from nowhere, even when it is direct. Direct traffic is when someone types in your blog address in a browser and lands on your website.

Before someone other than you or the creator would directly visit a website, you must have made an effort to send the person your blog address through some sort of advertising or promotion or awareness creation.

Another source of traffic is referral, which could come from social media or other websites. But the best source of traffic is the search engine, which one can refer to as organic, in the sense that they are natural, based on the content you have on your website. We will look at all these later.

5. Your name or brand should be well crafted

Have you come across those blogs whose names can't easily be pronounced? We all make mistakes by choosing discouraging names. If you have made a similar mistake just let the domain name expire and never renew again. Some names can be crafted to fit the niche. Simply looking at PerezHilton.com or AshleyMadison.com (the latter is not a blog) would make one want to visit the websites. Do not re-inforce failure. If your name isn't appealing, simply change it.

Perez Hilton is a crafted name used by the blogger – that's not his real name. Mario Armando Lavandeira, Jr. realized what a name Perez Hilton (a play on "Paris Hilton") was and how appealing it would be to people in love with celebrity news, and went ahead to blog with it.

You may even combine words. A blog about health, lifestyle and fashion I recently helped a client setup is named LifeStabilizer.com

You may think better names have all been registered and parked by businesses, but that's an illusion. Think of a great name after recognizing a niche you think you would thrive in.

Avoid a name that will limit you to a specific geographical location, unless your blog serves only the people of that area. For example, I would prefer to register the domain name KimKGossip.com to KimKGossipOnline.com or KimKGossipNY.com

Why would you attach online to a name when anything internet and blog is already online based. Many people make the mistake of attaching irrelevant words to a domain name. Avoid that! Those words include centre, update, online, blog, news (with the last two forgivable at times) etc.

Make sure your domain name reflects your website title. Don't register gossip.com and title your website My Gossip Centre! That could come as a subtitle though.

6. Website must be responsive

One of the major issues with Google's Blogger currently (as at the time of writing this) is that some of their templates are not responsive. When we talk about responsiveness, we refer to the ability of a website to adapt/fit to various screen widths.

The screen of many devices vary in width, and a website must adapt to those different screen widths for the best user experience. Wordpress has an edge over Blogger because of this responsiveness. Most Wordpress themes are responsive.

Why did I have to include this? Majority of the people visiting your blog are going to do so from a mobile device, and those mobile device will vary in screen width. If your blog does not respond to those variations, you are going to lose out because bad user experience may force your visitors to run away, even with the attractions you may already have in your website.

Google has a GoMo tool that can help analyze the way your website responds to mobile devices. Google will also rank websites that have mobile versions higher when searched from a mobile device.

If you are not sure of this, contact the person who designed your blog and make sure your blog looks great on mobile devices.

7. Sharing must be made easy

We are in a world where viral stuff become internet sensations. How do you think stuff go viral? It is by activities of others who share them. Your content can never be shared if you don't make sharing easy. Upworthy and Nova are good examples of sharing made easy blogs!

Never ignore any platform. Integrating sharing tools such as Addthis.com will make sure your users can share your content to any social media platform they use. Addthis has lots of other features you might end up enjoying. They will even let you know when any of your content is receiving a traffic spike!

Include sharing buttons close to the end of content – that's the ideal place to remind visitors to share.

Craft certain phrases that would make your visitors want to share. Examples are: Sharing is sexy! Sharing is Free! Don't be stingy, share! Nothing as noble as sharing! If you enjoyed this, your friends on Facebook may need it! Please share this to help others!

You should come up with better pleas to make them share!

Sharing buttons can even be made to pop up. But don't overdo this.

8. Comment is a must

I hate the feeling of reading news article from a website without a comment area – it's like walking alone through a desert! Don't ask readers to go to Facebook to comment, after reading on your website! That hurts!

Sometimes, I can jump to a YouTube video page for just one thing - to see what people are saying in the comment field. Comment is one of the few ways to give readers an opportunity to express their views on certain issues. I understand that some website owners, especially on Wordpress platform, disable comments due to spam.

If you are getting unrelated comments that advertise website links on a Wordpress comment, then you are probably not using Akismet. Captcha/ReCaptcha is also a way to reduce spam. Some websites just ignore comments to avoid abuses. You really need to do your best to avoid the abuse of your comment area, but that doesn't mean disabling comments entirely is the solution.

Integrating third party comments such as LiveFyre, Facebook Comments and Disqus could be a perfect way to reduce load on your server, provide good user experience and take advantage of the anti-spam systems already developed by those vendors.

One thing you must not do is to block a visitor's comment because it counters your view. It is their view, and as far as it doesn't break any rule, let it be. If you don't like it, make a rule and start implementing the rules for future comments.

Comment is a good way to keep visitors returning to your website, even to a page they have read before, just to reply to a comment. In the long run, you will see visitors even contributing more tips and facts than the original article through the comment section.

Never ever ignore the importance of comment. Some visitors are on your website to read comments, and not even your post. Comment is an organic content for you.

9. Be Present on Social media

In the early days of social media, several top websites ignored social media, mostly because these top websites enjoyed much traffic on their own platforms. But check what happens now, almost every reputable organization is on Facebook, Twitter, Instagram and Pinterest. Why the rush?

Social media presence gives businesses and organizations more reach to a wider audience, provide tools for customer service, and take the information you want to pass across to the visitors rather than the visitors coming for it.

Much like the RSS Feed, social media is another source blog posts get to fans, and interested fans most of the time return to the blog to find out more about the post. Social media can help with interacting with fans, and would even help you to get to know your fans better.

Social media will increase the worth of a blog, and in turn increase the income. This is how: A 5000/Day Visitor blog with a Facebook page of 1000 Likes is worth less than a 4000/Day Visitor blog with a Facebook page of 10,000 Likes. As long as these Facebook fans are real/active and are interested in the niche, and your blog sticks to the niche, the Facebook page will eventually provide traffic that will surpass the other blog with less Facebook Likes.

Some businesses would even prefer advertising with a blogger with more social media following, than another whose focus is just on his or her blog.

10. Search Engine must crawl frequently

When you search breaking news on Google, do you ever wonder why websites like CNN, BBC and co always come on top? It's actually not just because of good SEO (which shall be treated later), it's because Google has discovered that they have content related to the breaking news you searched for.

Other sites might have this breaking news, but their sites haven't been visited by Google's (Ro)bot or spider. Spider is a web crawler that visits a website and saves its content in a database to be used by search engines to learn what a website has and what it does not. It is through the crawled contents that Google is able to search through when you feed it a keyword. Some sites are crawled by Google once in a day, once a week, once a month or just three times in a year.

You can manually instruct Google bots to crawl your website or specific pages frequently. It can be hourly, daily, weekly, monthly or even yearly. You can do this through an XML sitemap. Find out more on Google Webmaster Tools for XML sitemap.

Remember, Google might end up not honoring your request if you set a frequency of "daily" for a specific page but the page is actually updated weekly. Set the crawl frequency to match your update frequency. Setting hourly frequency where it is not necessary will only add up to your server load, and with time, Google will learn to ignore your request.

11. Make it a business by monetizing

A blog is a hubby for some people and a means of income for others. In fact, majority are now going into blogging because of the ostensive lifestyle they see bloggers living. Bloggers like Perez Hilton and Linda Ikeji are multi millionaires, if not billionaires yet. There is no crime in hoping to get money from a blog, but many people make it the number one focus and forget to create content.

To make money from a blog, you have to monetize it. Monetization is actually the process of including sponsored contents otherwise known as advertising. Certain companies can pay for you to write about them. You can also put up banners that link to specific websites, and make money from the people you refer to those websites (affiliate marketing).

Some even make money from posting online surveys and polls on their website. Others make big money from replacing their background picture with the logo of certain companies, usually Heineken and Telecom giants.

But the surest way to earn money online is through Pay Per Click (PPC) and Pay Per view Advertising (PPV). Because to make money with these popular systems you either need views or clicks on some adverts, traffic becomes very important.

The Google Adsense program is an advertising service that lets bloggers and website owners monetize their content by pasting codes that show adverts according to their page's content (contextual) or visitor's interest (interest based). It is stress free, and that makes it the best.

12. AdSense is the best Ad Network, but not the only paying Ad Network

Google being a reputable company collects advertisements from businesses through the Google Adwords program and display those ads to publisher websites through the Google Adsense program. But just as Google don't accept all advertisements from advertisers, they also do not accept all publishers (bloggers who wish to join this great network). Getting an Adsense account has even become a business in the black market. New bloggers pay others in exchange for Adsense accounts because of the hassle involved in getting an Adsense Account.

I will show you the best and hassle-free way to get an Adsense account. It is as simple as creating a blog with a quality design and layout. Do everything this book already suggested by choosing a niche and creating original content. Make sure your content does not exist elsewhere, including pictures. You must have between 50-100 high quality and unique content on your blog. Submit your blog to Google.com/webmaster to make sure you get crawled. Monitor your traffic and make sure you are getting at least 100 unique visitors per day. Use Facebook to promote if you have no source of organic traffic.

Apply to Google Adsense and you will be accepted in a matter of days, taking note of their policy and making sure your blog does not violate any of those. However, if you have been blacklisted for any reason, or you weren't accepted, there are many alternatives.

Clicksor.com, Content.ad, Quadabra.com, Addynamo etc. Just Google (search on Google) *Adsense alternatives* and you will see loads of them. They will pay you, but not as much as Adsense. With time, you might even begin to accept advertisements directly, or try affiliate marketing. You can write about Amazon products in your niche, attach a product or category code or link and earn some commissions when you refer buyers to the e-commerce platform.

13. Learn to keep visitors

Keeping visitors on a website is an art that must be mastered. We have seen what bounce rate means in the traffic section. High Bounce rate is a menace to most bloggers. Bloggers spend a lot to drive traffic and still can't maintain steady traffic the moment they stop spending on traffic.

To leverage on new visitors, you must find a way to keep them engaged, and force them to try new pages. Please note that the more you keep them engaged, the less likely they are to click on an advert in the short term, but on the long term, they may return severally to click on several adverts or give you earnings through page views.

You can keep visitors from leaving by making sure that you encourage them to use the comment section.

You can keep them from leaving by making sure that there is a related content box just below the content. Some people go as far as monetizing the related part. Even Google Adsense has a related plugin that can help increase user engagement, but decrease your earnings as earlier mentioned.

You can also try and show pop ups when a reader gets to a certain area of the page, usually around the comment box. Inside the pop up, highlight other great content that you have.

It must not be related content; it could be trending or most popular content on your site. Wordpress has a plugin called Popular Post plugin. Blogger has that too.

Use them to reduce bounce rate and keep users engaged. But if your content is poor, the visitor may still be discouraged from trying more. So maintain a quality content archive and then use these tips to reduce bounce rate.

14. Don't expect to get rich overnight

We find people go into blogging with very high expectations, and these people often meet the opposite and give up. 90% of bloggers would probably give up before making $100 from the Adsense program. The 90% is just a guess, not an actual research statistics, but you may find out that more than that 90% actually give up when a real research is carried out.

The truth about blogging is that most people who made it big were those with willingness to keep pushing even without profit. Most of these were hobbyist bloggers who didn't even expect to earn a dime.

But because these popular bloggers like John Chow, Perez Hilton and Linda Ikeji have gotten extremely rich, so many enthusiasts get into the business with hope to get rich overnight. If you are one of those, you are living in illusion.

How can you suddenly get into this blogosphere and capture millions of traffic? Well, unless you have the money already to push into advertising, or you have been in the business of blogging. But as a newbie, it is impossible.

The best advice to a newbie blogger is to not expect any income from blogging for the first year of blogging. You may actually make money before the year runs out, but it is safer not to expect money. Within this time, focus on building huge followership, content and traffic. If you play your games well, you will soon get past this stage, and then start growing.

When you eventually start making money, never expect your income to grow forever. You will hit a stage when your income becomes static, fixated around a certain range. This is the stage when the intelligence of running a business is needed. You will really need to invest at this stage to grow further. We will discuss that later.

15. Events and seasons can inspire content

In the field of blogging, content is king as earlier mentioned. You will notice how some specific contents will draw traffic more than the others usually within a certain time. If you write about fashion and have written about winter clothes, there is a high probability that people will read the winter clothes article much more during the winter than in the summer.

If you write about agriculture, farming or gardening, there are seasons when planting is done, and that's when visitors would likely read what you post about planting. Get ready with posts about harvest at the right time.

Some events such as World Cup, Olympics and Celebrity Beef can inspire great content. Take for example a war started on Twitter by Kanye West when Wiz Khalifa wrote about KK. This inspired a lot of blog posts. Bloggers gain immense traffic from these kinds of events. Or was it when Kim Kardashian broke the internet? She really did if you know the traffic that brought to many publishers.

You must be able to monitor events and follow seasonal changes and let those inspire you to create great content. That's what blogging is all about – giving updates and not just writing feature articles. We will talks about feature articles later on.

16. Make use of Twitter Trending Hashtags

One of the most popular radar for detecting what event is heating up the internet is the Twitter Trends. When many people tweet with similar Hashtags and words within a short time, Twitter detects and groups these into trends.

#BringBackOurGirls

Who knew what it was all about? No one knew until we clicked on the Hashtag. So many persons tweeted with this hashtag when Boko Haram abducted about 270 girls from Chibok school and held them inside the Sambisa forest.

Donald Trump

Whenever people see this in trends, they assume something related to Donald J. Trump is trending and they would quickly click to see tweets about the American President.

People new to Twitter often find it difficult to understand what these trends do. But I have answered the question above. Apart from telling you what is currently heating up the internet, Twitter trends can inspire great content. Try and take advantage of it today.

17. Reddit can be good, as well as other forums

The front page of the internet, as it is referred to, Reddit.com is another place where internet sensations start. Any post that makes it to the front page of Reddit is enough to inspire you to write great content.

Posts get to the front page from the rate at which it is upvoted within a certain period of time. Posts on Reddit could be in the form of photos, videos or just text. The comment section is just another thing. Many bloggers just capture these and add their own opinion to create beautiful content for their visitors.

Depending on your niche, you can choose a particular subreddit (sub category on Reddit) and still be able to find great content to elaborate on, and create nice content.

Apart from Reddit, there are other forums where content can originate from, depending on which specific niche and location your blog serve. For Nigerians, never ignore Nairaland.com. For the United States, it's still Reddit. There are others too like 4chan.

18. Never give up when no one responds

There would be many times when you actually ask for people's opinion and you get no single feedback. This is no reason to believe that no one reads your blog. Understand that people are too busy and there are lots of content put in their face to consume daily. Apart from that, tech-saavy individuals tend to have preference to surf the internet incognito, especially when they are on non-established blogs. But you find them struggling to be the First to Comment on popular blogs. That's the way the world was wired.

If you can have any post whose major goal is to get feedback and you didn't get any feedback in 2 weeks, try republishing or unpublishing it; do the later only if the lack of feedback bothers you anyway.

But never assume no one saw the content because no one responded to it. I will show you how to find out if anyone actually saw the content later. But understand that no feedback does not translate to no traffic or no interest. A lot of persons surf the internet incognito, and would prefer to not leave a trace by dropping any form of feedback.

19. Invest to be seen and discovered

You have struggled to make sure people read your posts, but you still see many of your posts receiving very few impressions and no engagements. You are not alone. Many newbie bloggers get into this trap, usually because they didn't see the need to invest to be seen.

As already said, traffic does not come from nowhere; you must be willing to spend money initially. Spending to drive traffic is not something you just do to drive traffic in the short term and earn from Adsense, you have to have a long term plan. Your plan should be in such a way that even if you stop investing, the traffic generated from previous investments would become self-sustaining.

If you discover that for every 5000 visitors you get, you earn $20, your goal might quickly switch to making money instead of using some advertisement slots to promote your brand. If you promote your brand to these 5000 visitors, you may stand a chance to make extra $10 daily when they return the next day, without spending more on traffic. But if you focus on making money, you may earn $20 after spending $15 to drive traffic of 5000 visitors to your page on that day with no one returning the next day. Maybe you have even used the space meant for your logo to place an advertisement. There would be nothing to subconsciously make the visitor recognize the blog.

Your plan to drive traffic that guarantees return depends on what you advertise and where you advertise. We will look at Facebook and Twitter promotions.

20. Facebook Page promotion and post boosts

When we talk of investment, so many people do that on Facebook. They buy Likes which Facebook users offer for free. Yes, businesses and bloggers pay Facebook for Likes. I have seen some casual Facebook users believing that content owners earn when their content is liked; and I can understand where the confusion comes from.

It is also possible for Page owners to earn from advertisers depending on the number of Likes a sponsored post receives. But that arrangement is between the page owner and an advertiser.

You can promote a Facebook page by running a Facebook promotion. I have run some successful promotions where I spend close to $0.01 per Page Like. And since my Facebook page reflect the niche I'm in, whenever I post on the page, I get about 30% reach. Yes, Facebook won't show your posts to everyone that like your page, you have to put in more effort by boosting.

When you boost a Facebook post on your page, you pay Facebook to show the post to several people. That's why you see many posts with the word "Sponsored" on your Facebook feed. You can pay as little as $0.01 for every engagement, if you target well.

The best method to target and convert both in boosting and Page promotion is to target about 3 states/cities in a country, then target about 2 interests, and make sure your ads show only on feed of desktop and mobile device. Please ignore the Right Hand Side (RHS) or Right Sidebar Ads.

When a promotion takes off initially, the cost could be high. Just give it a day or two to start getting lower. Make sure to have a budget though, to avoid spending all your savings on Facebook because they will bill your credit card directly.

21. Twitter promotion and Hashtags

Often ignored in some quarters but if Twitter can drive traffic to a website based on trending hashtags, why can't it drive traffic when you promote on the platform. Twitter, even with declining earnings and struggling growth, is still the leader in micro blogging, and can fetch any blogger traffic in thousands.

We have talked about Trending Hashtags and how they can inspire you to write great content. Now is the time to tweet your post, and make sure you attach the hashtag.

"I appeal to Boko Haram to Please #BringBackOurGirls goog.hl/A3eYtm"

Since so many other people are viewing popular tweets in that trend, you might just end up getting retweeted and liked and getting thousands of traffic to your blog.

For promotion on Twitter, businesses go as far as paying for a hashtag to trend. You can also pay for a tweet to get seen and for your account to appear as sponsored, urging people to follow you. All these can be achieved for a low budget of up to $0.01 per engagement.

Because advertising on Twitter can be expensive some times, never let Twitter automatically set your CPC or CPM for you. Set what you are willing to pay and relax. When the budget of those bidding for higher CPC gets exhausted, they will fall back to your low budget. This is assured because the traffic on Twitter is likely more than the number of businesses willing to advertise on the platform.

You can always monitor your campaign on ads.twitter.com

22. ROI may be negative initially, but that won't last

Many would be pondering when bloggers would gain back the money spent in all the promotions, but I have no answer to that. Initially, return on investment (ROI) is expected to be negative. This means that in a certain month, a blogger could spend up to $500 on promotions, and make $400 back through the Adsense program. This is more than possible. This means a loss of $100.

One thing you will have to note is that if you keep spending on promotion and creating quality content, the loss would soon start to reduce and will eventually get to zero (0). This means you can spend $500 on promotions and gain around $500 back.

The next step would be to start making profit. If you stop promoting at this stage, it is possible to still make profit, but growth will never be guaranteed. Keep promoting and you will notice an increase in profit. You may spend $500 this month and make $700 back. Don't find the profit of $200 disgusting, it will still change.

Eventually, your profit could run into $1000 and then get to a point where profit will remain stagnant. That's a dangerous period. You will need to change several variables, especially your advertising budget. You will discover that as you increase the budget for advertising, earnings also go up.

There are other things you could do when you hit that static mark. We will discuss ways to increase earnings by changing certain variables later on.

23. Pay for safe traffic when necessary

Do you know that people create computer programs to surf a website and some analytics tool will record the page views? Yes, people create programs to send traffic to websites and you may find nothing wrong with this as long as you earn through page views or impressions. Well, ask yourself if you will find satisfaction in writing and believing people came to read your content, but in truth, only computer programs landed on the page. It is even worse for the advertisers on your page who don't get value for their money.

There are legitimate ways to seek and purchase real traffic and drive them to a website. While doing this, make sure the traffic comes from people who are interested in the content of the page and on the niche. These are what I would refer to as safe traffic. Don't force people to visit your blog by redirecting them from an external source.

You can purchase safe traffic from forums, Facebook Pages and Facebook groups. Just make sure they are coming with the knowledge of what the page is all about. Don't promise to Get them a Free Visa to the US and then land them on a page talking about women health.

24. Avoid spamming

Frustration from traffic can lead one to try several options, including gathering emails, joining forums and pasting links to blog pages everywhere. Have you ever been in a forum where the topic is about Tech gadget, and then one marketer joins and suddenly starts posting about how Kim Kardashian has broken the internet and torn it apart with her naked and butt pictures? Or about how El-Chapo, the Mexican drug lord escaped prison for a record third time? These are perfect examples of spamming.

Another form of spamming is by sending marketing emails to people who didn't subscribe to your content, and still not even giving them a way out. Some people can be that heartless to tag even a priest on a Facebook post about how Kim Kardashian's sextape was played at Wiz Khalifa's concert in Brazil. Avoid tagging people that would be uninterested in what you post on Facebook. Tagging should only be done when you are sure the person would be very interested in the content you shared.

In fact, spamming is a crime if you do not know, depending on where you are. The least you can do is post on your Facebook timeline and let your friends who are not interested start to unfollow your posts. But avoid tagging people in posts that wouldn't be of interest to them. Instead, create a Facebook page or Group on your niche and start posting there. You will be surprised that people who value your content will start joining your community and help you fulfill your traffic goals.

25. Never ignore professional advice and service

You find people with no experience of the internet setting up blogs themselves, installing loads of plugins, designing logo, choosing layout and what not? They are master of all trades, and believe they are saving costs.

The truth is that unprofessionalism speaks for itself just as professionalism does too. Simply loading a mediocre blog on a browser, even with the right content will make some people purge. A poorly designed logo is enough to make a professional doubt the validity of a very correct article on a web-page, except in few cases where the websites belong to popular institutions and organizations. Start patronizing professionals. Fiverr is an example of a place to get professionals.

Some people involve professionals right from the stage of choosing a domain name, choosing a hosting provider, choosing the right platform, and choosing a marketing strategy. Others ignore this and take the journey on their own. It could be to save cost but think about the cost that would be saved on the long run.

A professional will know what database to backup before doing a major upgrade but a mediocre blogger will make changes that will crash the entire blog, and then end up deleting the database hoping to roll back changes. This in turn deletes the entire blog and forces the blogger out of business.

Yes, that's how some blogs were killed!

26. Let a web designer give you the best layout

Because you are using Wordpress does not give you the authority to make choice of a theme you like. It's not just about what you like but what would help you achieve business goals. Website layout or theme in the case of Wordpress can say a lot about what your goals are.

If you include Ads in sidebars or above the fold, it might mean you want visitors to see the Ads more while giving them chance to read the content. Those are actually not the best place for clicks, to increase CTR.

To increase CTR, you have to embed Ads within content or at the end of content. Most visitors to a website would click on adverts just after reading the article or consuming any content on the page. But you find out that a lot other actions compete for space just under the content. These are comments, sharing buttons, email newsletter subscription and then the advert. You have to prioritize thus:

Embed Ads before the last paragraph, add sharing button immediately after the content, include another Ads, add the comment box, and then one more Ads. This is the perfect way to position all three Adsense for Content Ads on a page for the best CTR.

If you have no sidebars, then probably you want a non-distractive reading. If you include related after the content, then you are reducing the probability of a visitor taking one of the following actions: Click an ads, share the content or add comment.

Some would even remove other distraction and attach only Ads at the end of the content, to make sure CTR is high. You will learn more about CTR and CPC later.

27. Learn basic HTML

`<b>Why am I bold?</b>`

The HTML code above can still be achieved by highlighting the text and hitting CTRL+B. But learning the basic way to achieve these could be of much advantage. In the earlier days of Wordpress, some bloggers found it difficult to embed a YouTube video without the help of plugins. We still find some bloggers paste HTML codes in fields meant for rich text editing. This outputs strange characters to visitors. This simply happens because the blogger lacks the knowledge of Basic HTML.

HTML which stands for Hyper Text Markup Language is the language of the web. It is styled with CSS, but you don't need to go that far. With HTML, you can do several things your normal Rich Text Editor is incapable of doing.

Assuming you have a YouTube video on a page and the embed code you pasted has an attribute of a fixed width:

```
<embed src="url of the video" width="500px"></embed>
```

This video might have issues with mobile devices of width smaller than 500 pixels. But with proper HTML knowledge, you can tweak the code to have width="100%" which makes it fluid and fit for any width.

This same thing could be done with images/pictures.

```
<img src="url of picture" width="500px"/>
```

could turn to

```
<img src="url of picture" width="100%"/> or
<img src="url of picture" style="width:100%;height:auto;"/>
```

The latter is CSS and is even a better way of coding, but you are a blogger so you may choose to ignore. More HTML tags can be found when you Google.

28. Keep in touch with your audience, but watch it

Once in a while, try to be active in your own comment section. When someone writes a comment, take some time out to respond to the comment. Even Facebook CEO Mark Zuckerberg responds to comments on his posts. Why not you? You are too busy?

You are not a robot and your readers know that. The best you can do to keep them returning and even establish a relationship with them is to keep in touch through comments. You will detect faster when anything is broken if you use all the features meant for visitors in your blog. Assuming you have been monitoring a specific user named Mike who comments all the time and suddenly Mike stops commenting. If Mike happens to return after a week or a month to comment, respond with "Hey Mike, longest time. How are you doing?" You will discover that Mike will be pleased with the fact that you have been taking note of his contribution and that you missed him while he was away.

Avoid countering their opinions on sensitive matters. If Angela commented on how Kanye West should be stoned because of what he said about Amber Rose, simply use an emoji to respond. You don't have to say anything to that. You may choose to ignore too.

Avoid getting into arguments with your readers. A single response is enough per person per post. Any more follow up has a potential of turning into a disaster.

29. Offer giveaways to keep them coming back

A post gets an average of 50 comments on a certain blog, and that's high. One day, the blogger decided to create a post thus:

> **January Giveaway**
>
> I made so much progress last year and would like to give back to this community. You guys have been so helpful. I want to share $1,000 to 5 readers. Each lucky reader will get $200. Please comment with your email address or phone number and you will be reached if you win.
>
> The winners would be:
>
> 1st Comment
>
> 55th Comment
>
> 201st Comment
>
> 700th Comment
>
> 1000th Comment

This blog that receives an average of 50 comments per post in its lifetime received about 2000 comments on this post in less than 15 hours.

There is power in giveaways. People love to receive, and it must not be cash money! I won't say more.

30. Avoid fake news, but label rumor when not sure

When CNN report something, people tend to believe it more before even confirming. But when TMZ or MediaTakeOut says something, it is regarded as 80% fake news pending confirmation.

Do you know how many times Rihanna has gotten pregnant in the world of fake news? Do you know how many times Kim Kardashian and Kanye West have divorced? What of Kylie Jenner and Tyga? These blogs are a joke most of the time.

Do you wish to have credibility for whatever you report and still be able to drive traffic from whatever trends? Try to avoid fake news or label as "Rumor" if you must post them.

Rumor: Donald Trump Not Fit To Be US President according to latest investigations.

That headline, even though it looks like a joke, the first word will justify and give you some credibility. Goal.com does this all the time with their transfer news rumour.

Humor: Rihanna is pregnant again, for the record 10th time, according to TMZ

How about that tweak? It's humor and a mere joke, but you can use that to drive traffic. Humor me on what bloggers do for traffic.

31. Make sure you have other things doing

You may decide to research on other businesses such as e-commerce, website design, consultancy etc. Offer other services because blogging could crumble any second as a career due to certain constraints.

I've seen people whose means of income died the day they were banned from the Google Adsense program.

I have also seen people who gave up blogging because blogger.com closed down their blog for policy violation issues.

If all your eggs are in the basket of blogging and anything like that happens, what would you fall back to? Make sure to have other things doing, especially as a newbie blogger. Don't quit your job so you can start blogging.

You can combine the two and finally quit when blogging begins to pay steadily. But still, think of other things to do.

32. Use sticky note and Write Space Chrome App to keep reminders

There is this Google Chrome app called Write Space that behaves much like the Sticky Note on windows. There is always need to type and save stuff while blogging. It could be future post suggestions or things you need to do later, after blogging. Having these tools can save you time of leaving your browser to search for stuff or to take notes.

To use the Chrome App, just open a new tab and go to Apps. But you must have the Write Space installed. Find the link to the ChromeStore at the bottom right of the photo below or simply search for that word on Google.

33. Remember to have friends to talk to when your head starts misbehaving

Yes, this is very important. Monotony can be tiring at times. There are days when you may not have much to post or when you may be too bored to write. You are not the only one who gets to this state of mind. Just find other things to do.

Bloggers don't have time. If they are not writing, they are reading. If they want to rest, they start chatting on their phones. Even playing a computer game could be tiring at times, but it does help relieve stress.

In times like this, you really need to take a walk away from a computer, meet someone and spend some time talking about other things, drinking, watching a movie or even going to a swimming pool.

34. Use Google Analytics to monitor progress

Never ignore the importance of metrics. These will help you understand if really you are making progress or not. Jay Z once said that people may lie, "but numbers never lie." Bill Gates acknowledged the importance of accurate data when he pointed out that Africa's Richest man, Aliko Dangote, did not get rich by pretending to sell bags of cement he never had. "I took from that that while it may be important to be polite, it's more important to face facts so that you can make progress," according to Bill Gates.

Google has a very important analytics tool and a good academy for you to learn how to use them. Google the words "Google analytics academy" to get started.

With Google Analytics, you can watch how your visitors interact with your blog pages, set goals and see how those goals are converting. You can use the realtime tab to see the number of visitors currently on your blog, where they are from, who referred them, what platform they are on, and several other details.

You can also use the tool to monitor page views, sessions and users. A user counts as a device on this analytics platform. If I visit your blog with a mobile phone and then return again from a computer, this counts as two different users. A session is like a group of page views from a particular user within a short period of time. A session usually expires after around 20-30 minutes of inactivity. A user can contribute to more than one session when he or she returns to your blog severally within a day. As per page views, this counts as the number of pages opened by any visitor irrespective of whether the user or session has been on the page before. There is also a unique page views metric where only the first visit on a page from a user per session is counted. Others hits on that same page are ignored.

There are lots more you can learn with the analytics tool and we will treat some in detail later. But understand that accurate data will lead to growth.

35. Know what your readers expect from search

If you have checked the Google analytics tool, then you will notice that you can actually track what your readers expect from you. It is important that every blog must have a search field to aid in content discovery. This search field does not only help your visitors, it equally helps you.

You can setup Google Analytics to help track what people search for on your site by going to Admin and view settings. Enable search tracking and include a search parameter. The best parameter is usually the letter "q" so that searches are appended in the url of your blog as follows:

Blogaddress.com/search/?q=Help+Article

In a typical Wordpress site, the search parameter is the letter "s".

Blogaddress.com/?s=Help+Article

The + you see is a special character that stands for space. Read up on *url encoding* to clear any confusion about this. You may also need a professional to help you set this up. To monitor what people search for on your site, just go to Google Analytics, Click on Behaviour and then browse to Search Terms.

You will see people searching for things your website should actually have dedicated pages on, but maybe you didn't remember to write about them. Never ignore the importance of getting writing tips from the searches.

36. Give them a contact page

Apart from searching for content on your blog and being able to comment on posts, you must also give your readers a means to contact you whenever they have to. You will notice that some will even submit content to you, make very useful suggestions and give tips. But don't expect the messages to be all good. Some could be abusive, and you may just need to ignore.

If you find any serious threat from these messages, don't fail to contact the police.

The contact page could be just email and phone number. You can use Captcha to reveal them, to reduce abuse/spam.

37. Do guest posts or sponsored posts

All the content on your blog must not be from you. You may decide to post for people and charge them or even do a cross-partnership where you exchange articles and link back to the author's website. This could help enlarge networks, increase search engine ranking and fetch some visitors.

Sponsored posts can also be a major means of income. You can even do a post about a particular product or service, put an affiliate link on the post and make money each time it converts. You can do that with web hosting platforms, domain name registrars, Amazon products, traffic providers like MaxVisit etc.

Please think about quality while doing this and don't overdo it. Take at most one sponsored or guest post after every five (5) posts from you. That 5:1 ratio is the minimum you should be able to accept. Anything below that is excessive and might impact on your readers who will no longer see reasonable posts. 10:1 ratio is recommended. This means you have to make 10 posts before you make a sponsored post.

38. You must have a frequency at which you post

People will often return to your website if you noticed from the Google Analytics tool. There are always returning users and new users. Returning users are coming back either because they expect to find something new or because they were referred back from search engine or social media.

Visitors who find your content useful will most likely return expecting to find something great. Do not disappoint them. As a blogger, you must have something new after a certain period of time. It could be hourly, daily, twice in a week, thrice in a week, weekly, monthly etc.

When you disappoint from your usual frequency, you will not only be scaring your readers, you will also be scaring the search engine robot or spider that crawls your site with a certain frequency.

Instead of disappoint, use schedule to make sure posts follow the normal frequency. We will talk about automatic scheduling of posts later on.

39. Give a surprise post every once in a while

Bloggers are humans and have certain weird interests outside their niche. Use this to deliver a surprise sometimes. But please do this at most once in a month to avoid abuse.

A blogger whose niche is fashion could decide to post something from a football match won. This blogger is a Chelsea football Club fan and they haven't won a match in their last 5 games. Then Chelsea FC eventually won a match. It would look weird to post such on a fashion blog, but let your fans know that you are a Chelsea fan and that the win was so important to you and you need them to rejoice with you.

Some will call you silly for posting that. Others will throw a joke. But majority will tell you about their football taste too.

40. Title isn't all you need if you care for your future

Title says a lot. In fact, it takes a good marketer to construct a good title. But in as much as you need to sell your content through the title, you still owe your readers an explanation for the title, which they must see in the content. The content must make effort to convince them that the title made sense.

If you said that someone dropped a nude photo and it turns out it was just a bikini photo, you may end up losing clicks to your blog in the future because they will remember the name of your blog for that fake promise, and never click on anything that emanates from it in the future. Now does my title make sense? Title isn't all you need if you care for your future.

You will craft your title to attract, take as many pages as you may want to, but make sure you keep to your promise.

Photo: Rihanna does it again

Make sure there is a strange photo on that page that shows Rihanna, or an event that you will narrate. It must convince the reader that Rihanna has done something again. Wait, she must have done it before! You need to prove that too.

41.   Follow the rules and don't show nudity

When Google Adsense says you are not allowed to show their advertisements on pages containing nudity, this is what they mean:

If your post has a photo that shows nudity, either remove advertisement from that particular page, or remove the photo or even the post entirely. It is not enough to claim to censor the picture – you would still get banned if they fish you out.

There are more rules like not asking people to click on the advertisements to prove their support. Make sure you read their policy and follow the rules.

Even linking to a porn site is a violation when Adsense code is on your page. Avoid these and Adsense will never ban you from their program.

42. Join blogger Groups

You never know what new tip is working for bloggers, or what new Wordpress plugin will help you achieve some goals. When you interact with other bloggers, you will discover ways to help one another.

Bloggers have groups on Whatsapp, BBM, Facebook and even on popular forums. You need to join these forums to learn more on upgrading your skills with whatever is in vogue.

43. Do not copy and paste. Rewrite or seek permission

You find many bloggers copying and pasting exactly what is on other websites, without permission. Even though this practice is frowned upon, people still do it, including popular blogs that serve as role models in certain countries.

There are many ways you can write your own version of a particular news article. As a blogger, I do not mean that you should run down to Syria and get the original photos and conduct the interview – that's for journalists. But you have a responsibility to not paste exactly what another site published, starting from titles and content and photos. Unfortunately, you find people do this.

There is this popular Wordpress plugin called RSS post importer. People use it to import content from other Wordpress or Blogger websites through RSS feeds. This isn't a good idea. Even when you use the plugin to import content, don't publish it without editing.

Editing starts from the title. Change the title by reading the content. There are many other headlines you can make from the content. Also paraphrase the content and use quotes to show areas you copied verbatim. Give proper attribution like "according to CNN". Yeah, that helps.

It is also a good idea to write whoever you are copying from to obtain permission before publishing on your own blog. This will even save you from getting banned by Adsense, if you use the program.

44. Take a break for your health and eyes

Do you know that working for long hour can cause you some health issues? Staring on a computer screen as bloggers do for long hours can hurt the eyes. Sitting on a certain position for long hours can cause varicose veins and some other health complications. You don't have to work for that long, learn to take a break.

I will leave you with this wonderful quote from Dalai Lama:

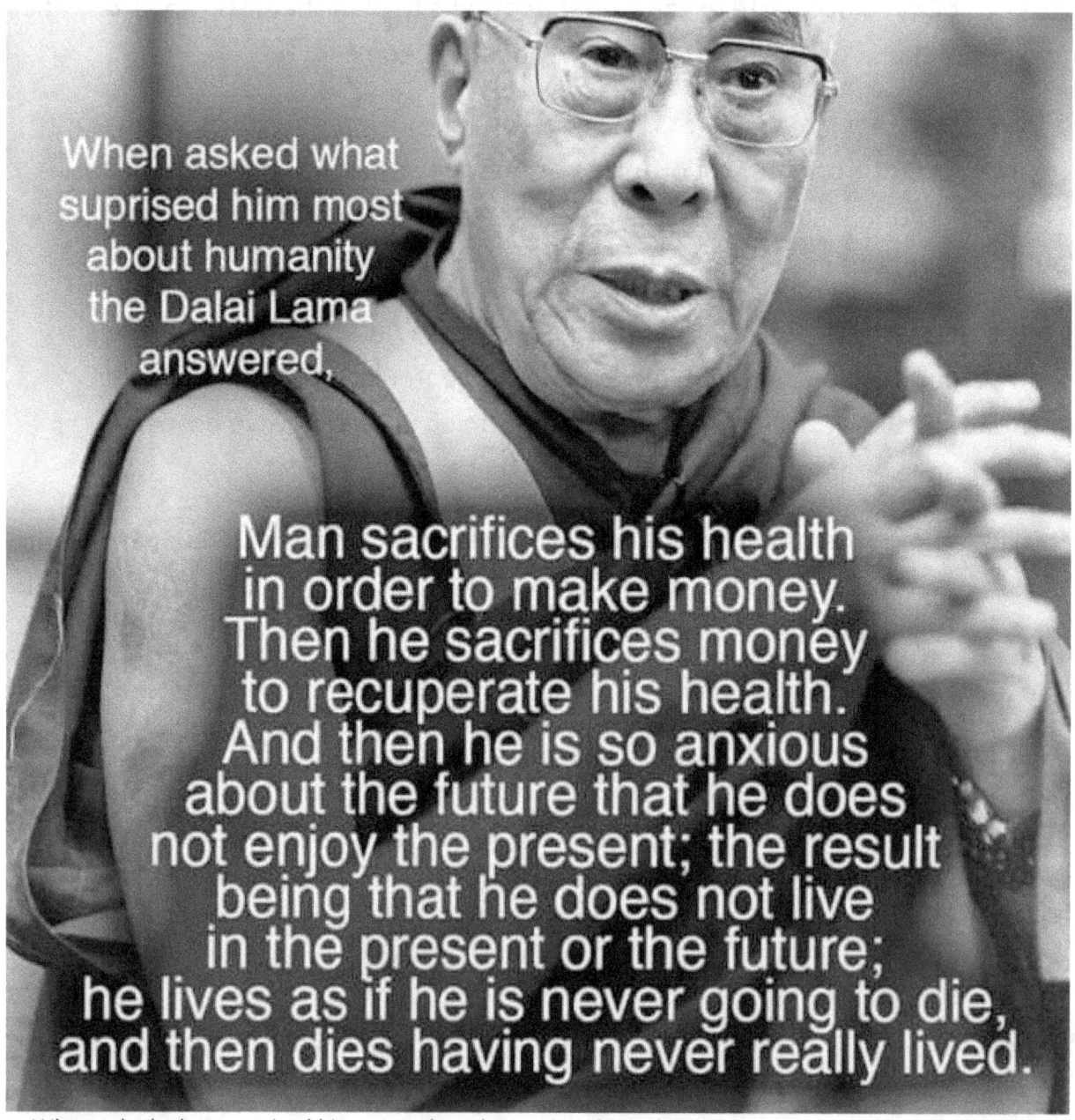

When asked what surprised him most about humanity, the Dalai Lama answered: Man sacrifices his

health in order to make money. Then he sacrifices money to recuperate his health. And then he is so anxious about the future that he does not enjoy the present; the result being that he does not live in the present or in the future; he lives as if he is never going to die, and then dies having never really lived.

45. Use Google trends and YouTube's

Just like the Twitter trends, Google has a trend of popular searches that can help inspire you on what to post. They also have a trend of what most people are watching on YouTube. Take a look at the screenshots below:

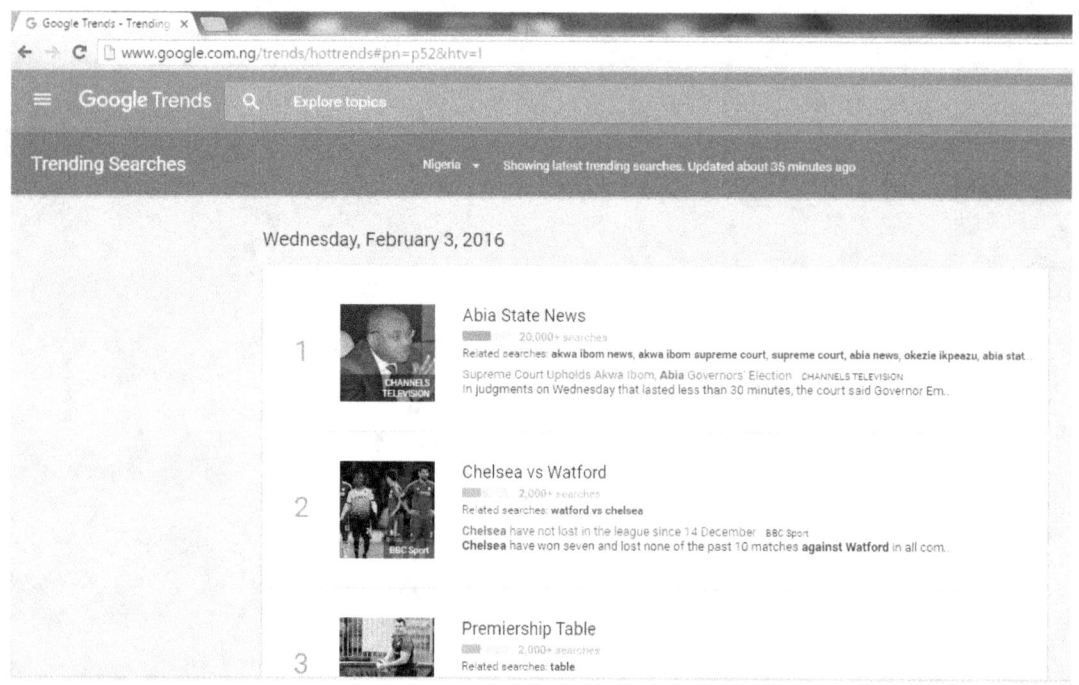

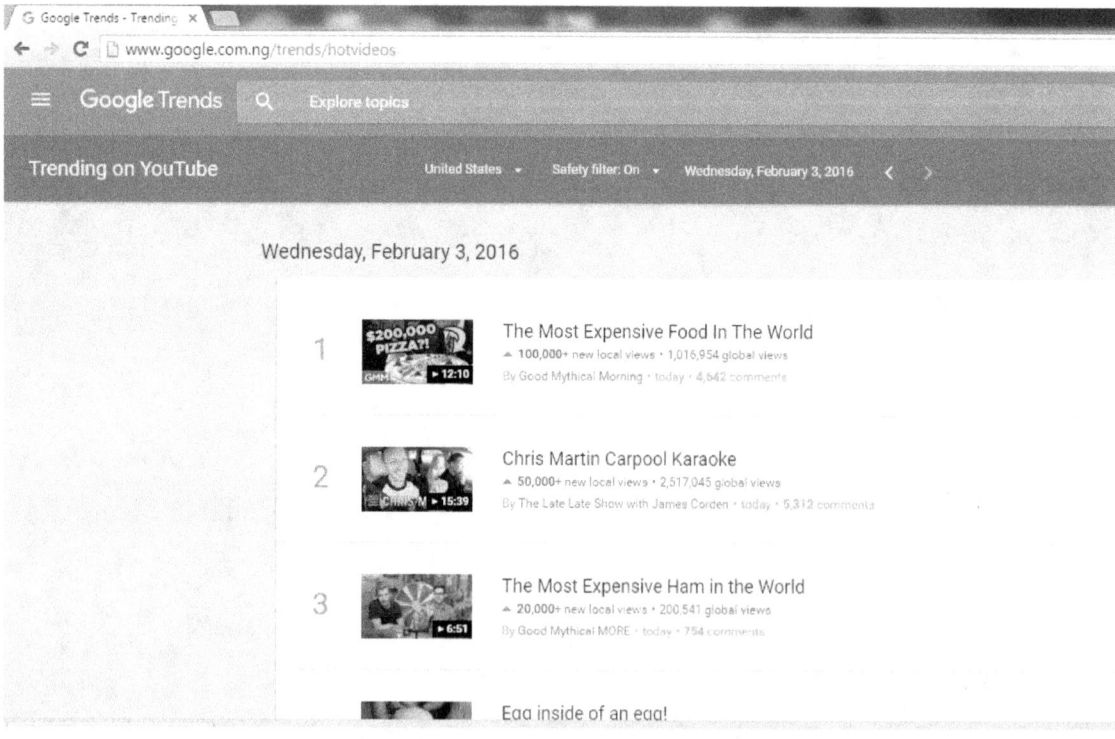

46. Be funny sometimes or post funny YouTube

You really need to be funny in your posts or at least have a little sense of humour. It can be forgiven if you are not funny, but what can't be forgiven is not being able to find a way to make your reader laugh. Even a single "Caption this" photo is enough post to make people laugh. Try to include these.

YouTube has loads of comic videos uploaded daily. The YouTube Trend is a good place to discover latest funny videos. Make sure to make at least one funny post every day.

47. Don't be a sexist with he or she

Some people fall prey to turning sexists while writing a blog post. They either assume everyone is either male, while others assume everyone is a female. Take a look at these:

> "If a stranger walks up to you in the church to demand for your phone number, what would you tell him?"

If that's the case, then the sentence should read:

> "If a strange man walks up to you in the church to demand for your phone number, what would you tell him?"

And if you didn't want to talk about a specific gender, then try:

> "If a stranger walks up to you in the church to demand for your phone number, what would you tell him or her?"

Avoid using "he" alone or "she" alone where you aren't actually referring to a specific gender. Instead use "she" or "he" or "s/he".

And never assume every engineer is a man or every nurse a woman.

48. Don't bare it all in the title

Long titles are fine but what's the use if you succeed in revealing all the goodies in the title? Titles are meant to be appealing and attractive to click assuming you find them on Facebook. Titles can help drive traffic to your website.

> A popular footballer just died – find out who!

This title may just be too serious for any football lover to ignore. But with a name mentioned, you may find out that clicks to the page will surely be reduced. Avoid revealing all the information in the title.

While doing this, remember not to misuse it and fill the title with fake promises as already treated.

Checkout Upworthy.com for the best title tips. Reading their news will give you a tip on how to write attractive titles.

49. Know when your readers expect to find and schedule

With tools like Facebook insight, you are likely to know when most of your posts are seen on Facebook. Some bloggers may rush to post news in the morning thinking that's the best time to be read. But statistics may suggest otherwise. You may notice that most of your readers are active only around evening and night time. To take advantage of this, what you need to do is post according to their schedule.

If your schedule will not allow you to post according to the time your readers are active, use **post schedule** to schedule posts. Wordpress and Blogger have schedule tools that would be very helpful. You can even schedule posts for a full day and take a break that day. That's why blogging gives liberty if you really need to be free.

50. Blend to holidays and events

Still on proper communication with fans and visitors and making the person behind a blog seem human, make sure to post season's greeting during popular seasons such as New Year, Christmas, Easter, New Months, Valentine, Thanksgiving etc.

Add a Santa Claus hat to your logo during Christmas, change your background to a scary costume during Halloween and remember to wish your readers well.

You can even post photos from your vacation.

51. Avoid getting into a fight in the comment section

As already advised, avoid responding more than once to a comment as that could spiral into argument, name calling etc. as we see celebrities do on Instagram daily. Several celebrities tend to forget that if they are to become role models, they must learn to ignore certain comments left on their Instagram photos by fans. When you don't know that you are a role model, anger will get the best of you.

If someone comments on your blog and you deem the comment abusive, you do not need to respond to the person, simply use your super power to delete the comment. This is why you must have the privileges to moderate the comment section in whatever blogging platform you use.

Fans or readers are allowed to fight with one another in the comment section as we find on YouTube videos all the time, but not the OP. Your duty is to moderate or simply ignore insulting comments that target you directly.

52. Give career tips and not just news that keep readers all day

Do you know that certain people wake up in the morning, take their phones and start browsing the internet, and they do that until sun set? Do you think people who do this, even if they will be on your blog all day, are doing well for themselves? Definitely not.

There are certain career posts that you can make and they will be a turning point for a certain reader who has nothing else to do other than browse the web all day. As someone who tells a story to several people, you have a power to convince certain people to follow a certain path, and you have a responsibility to advise them to be useful to themselves and the society, just as you are with your blog.

If your niche is about fashion, you can post opportunities in the fashion field such as learning to become a fashion designer, applying to modeling agencies, selling clothes on e-commerce websites etc. In as much as you need to market your blog and make money, you will record greater testimonies from helping your readers become useful to themselves and the society.

I was reading a blog the other day when I discovered Fulfillment by Amazon (FBA). This kind of tip could be the U-turn for that internet savvy fan who has no way to make money on the internet. You can go ahead and Google that "FBA". The killer tip is to import from Aliexpress, ship to Amazon warehouse direct and sell at twice the price of purchase. There are many cheap unbranded China products that you can even sell x3 of the cost price and it would still be cheap in the US.

53. Repost feature posts when you are too busy

As a blogger, you don't have to be in the business of writing all the time. There are posts whose value don't diminish with time. A news article about "How Lucky Dube Died" would be useless to republish again. But an article about "How to prevent varicose veins" can be published at least once every month and still be relevant even in the next 10 years. These kinds of posts are known as feature posts and are meant to be saved in specific categories.

When you need to take a break, it would be nice to re-schedule the feature posts to be re-published again. This keeps the blog busy and makes sure new visitors find interesting content.

Most helpful tips are feature posts.

54. Readers should be aware whenever you are away

There are times when you will have engagements to attend, but readers want something to read. You know you do have something for them to read right there? As a blogger, you can post, letting them know that you will be away for a certain number of days or hours etc. Promise to update or let them know that you have scheduled some useful posts within the time you will be away.

That should help in keeping the traffic you receive constant or growing. If you don't do this, you may start noticing traffic decline because some may even think you have gone out of business and would simply remove your blog from their bookmarks.

55. Apologize whenever you make a mistake

It is OK to make mistake, that's why we've been stressing that bloggers are not robots or computers, but human. But what readers can't tolerate is a blogger whom when called out for a mistake would decide to either ignore or cover up.

When you are wrong, you are wrong. Owning the platform does not give you the right to be infallible. Have you not seen big brands like Coca-Cola and Toyota apologizing to customers for simple mistakes? Who are you not to accept that you are wrong?

You can post a false story and when that story is proven to be false, don't stick to correcting the title by adding rumor or editing. Simply attach an apology and reference the error.

Sometimes you can make a grammatical error and a reader might correct you in comments, acknowledge the correction and edit. Please be careful not to be confused into writing rubbish all in the name of correction. Use your sense to know what is right and wrong while taking corrections.

When you make a joke about sensitive event, apologize. When you are found in the most unlikely places, supporting the wrong causes or found disobeying civil laws, and the story makes it out to the public, apologize because certain people look up to you on your blog.

56. Viral lie can fetch traffic, but won't keep traffic

We all know how we want to be the first to break the news about Beyonce breaking up with Jay Z. Hmmm, something foul smells here. How did you get that story? You chat with Jay Z on Whatsapp and he told you that.

You want to run a viral story that can fetch you a lot of traffic. Think about how the viral news would make serious internet users hate your site and make them vow never to click a link with trace to your blog name.

Viral lie is going to fetch you the traffic you need, but won't keep the traffic coming. Have some credibility and avoid gaining fame through the back door. Fake news is a crime!

57. Watch your CPC and CTR

Remember when I said "Every blog must have a niche and your niche has a lot to do with how successful you are going to be in your new field" ? I meant it. Your niche will play a key role in your CPC and your CTR. CPC means Cost per click and is the amount an advertiser pays you per single click on an advert. When contextual Ads are shown, they are made to be relevant to one's content and the CPC will vary.

If your page talks about fashion, you will possibly see an Aliexpress, Jumia or any of the popular e-commerce sites Ads on your page. These Ads pay as little as 1 cent when clicked, because of what its conversion could mean for the seller. They may pay as high as $1 per click, but the CPC is usually very low. This same applies to relationship, dating etc.

But those in the automobile niche, insurance, student loans, banking and even law will have a different story. Some Ads in this category can pay as high as $100 per click because of what a conversion could mean for the advertiser. A single click can fetch the advertiser thousands of dollars if the visitor is genuinely interested in the product.

You can use keyword research tools to find out which niche keywords pay higher.

CTR means Click Through Rate, and this is a measure of how many clicks an advert receives per 100 page views (with ads shown). Sometimes, CTR can be as low as 0% and as high as 100%. But remember that as your page views increase, CTR is likely to fall. When your daily page view is less than 1000, your CTR should be up to 2%. However, as the page views go higher, expect a slightly lower CTR. When your CTR falls below 0.5%, it is possible you are doing something wrong with Ads Layout. If Ads layout is fine, then your niche probably attracts people with knowledge of what Ads are and those people know how to avoid Ads. This happens mostly in Technology and blogging niche. You only receive clicks when they think you've been helpful and want to support.

You will learn more about optimizing Layout for best CTR later on.

58. Take a crash course on writing or see how others write

A course on writing isn't a bad idea if you are new to blogging. You find people who don't know the difference between "You're" and "Your" not to talk of "I'm" and "Am". Some bloggers while typing forget that there must be a space after certain punctuations such as full stop (.), Comma (,), exclamation mark (!), question mark (?), colon (:), semi-colon (;) etc.

> There are indications that Donald Trump May Win.What do you think?Let me Know.

When people type like this, some programs will think there is a website address in this string of text called "Win.what"

> There are indications that Donald Trump May Win. What do you think? Let me Know.

You see the difference? The spacing can help a lot. However, when using dash to join two words, there is no need for spacing. Cat-fish should not be turned to "Cat- Fish" because of the rule on spacing after punctuation.

Take a crash course on writing and you should be ready to write professionally.

59. Unless you are a CNN type, write briefly

You must understand that as a newbie blogger, you shouldn't make your news the same length with what CNN and BBC publish. People will not have the time to read all that. If they will have the time, they may prefer to visit the original source of the news to read first-hand material.

Try as much as you can to read and summarize before posting. Short posts will be more useful unless you are writing a useful article. But if you are reporting breaking news, make it short and straight to the point.

The only time you need to give an explanation is when you need an explanation.

60. Don't market irrelevant stuff. Turn them down

Some people publish content that are irrelevant to what their blog represents all in a bid to make money. Imagine a health and lifestyle blog talking about SEO and linking to an Indian based SEO Company. That's too weird please.

The marketing posts you receive must somehow be in tune with your niche or at least be related. When you receive a song from a friend to be published on an insurance blog, please turn it down. Forget the surprise I talked about in a previous chapter, unless the song is from you. Reject unrelated sponsored posting especially when your blog is in a professional niche.

REJECT! REJECT!! REJECT!!!

If they insist with a better offer, then turn me down and accept. Always weigh the impact the post might have on your professional audience. It is fine to accept just anything for banner Ads, but not for sponsored posts.

61. Research before you post on topics you are not sure about

You have probably seen some of those warnings about how NASA warned that an asteroid would hit the earth and cause a huge blast that will cover the atmosphere with dust for decades. There are possibilities that this could happen, but why say NASA said so? You probably found the news on a blog with very low credibility.

There is need to research before posting about some things. Never assume you know everything about a specific subject. Let me share an example of what happened to Donald trump with you:

 Wale Gates @walegates · 5h
According to Donald Trump.... Paris is in Germany.... bet he can see Mexico from his garden...

 **Donald J. Trump**
@realDonaldTrump

Man shot inside Paris police station. Just announced that terror threat is at highest level. Germany is a total mess-big crime. GET SMART!

RETWEETS   LIKES
4,665   5,251

1:24 PM - 7 Jan 2016

Who do you think made the mistake? Was it that Trump needed to research on Geography before making that tweet or did Wale fail to comprehend? Be the judge. But the point is to research before you jump into conclusion.

62. Don't do news about your family unless you are a Kardashian

Even the story of the Kardashians bore me a times. Why should even their private lifestyle become a story? But there are people interested in knowing what's up with every member of the Kardashian family. But just because people follow the story of this great American family does not mean yours will be followed. Don't make your blog about members of your family because you will eventually bore out any reader you have.

Even readers of Linda Ikeji Blog complain when she posts about her sister who is into modeling. And you think telling your readers that *your younger brother who was in Afghanistan returned* would become an internet sensation. Please, focus on your niche. If you have nothing to post about, maybe it's time to take a nap until something else trends on Twitter?

63. Show ads within post

One of the greatest ways to mask Ads and make them seem like part of the content is to embed them in a post. Apart from the three Adsense for Content I talked about in layout, there are other three Ads you can include which are known as text-based Ads or Link Box. Link box Ads are formed from the content of your page. If a page is about a new music from Rihanna and how you can download them for free on Tidal, you will find the link-box ads change to something like:

Download Music from Rihanna

Rihanna's music

Get song from Tidal

Why won't a visitor click on those Ads after consuming the content of the page? They are contextual. In fact, you can also click on Link Ads. Yes, they are the only Ads you are allowed to click because they end up showing a search page with more Ads relevant to the user.

You can embed these after each paragraph, up to three paragraphs and you will see your CTR improve. The only issues I have noticed with Link Ads is that they will promise and fail. You may click on the "Get song from Tidal" link and end up on a page with adverts about dating. See what you were promised? See what you got?

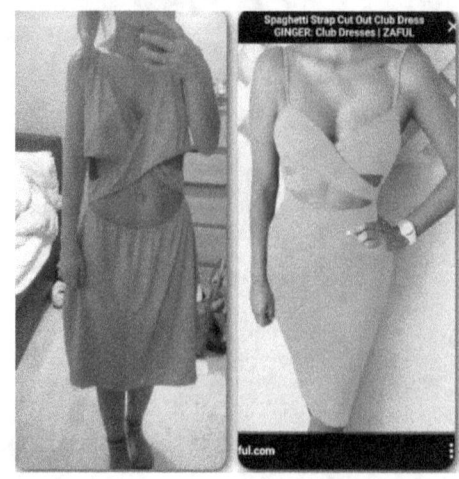

64. Break long posts to gain from page views

This is a very useful thing to do because you don't only earn revenue from clicks on adverts, you earn from views too. To inflate views, the smart way is to split some content into multiple pages. The kind of posts that do well with this are stuff like "Top 10 tricks to do this" or "10 most Handsome Celebrity Boyfriends" etc.

You can keep each on a page, then link it to the others in such a way that the visitor has to browse across all the pages to find all the information that he or she might need.

You can also do this with helpful articles such as: "5 Reasons Why This Happens", "10 steps to financial stability", "20 tips to send your blog to the next level" and you will see people who actually need the information browse across 20 pages, giving you extra revenue from views and even reducing your bounce rate.

You can also do this with photos from celebrities. Assuming Amber Rose or Kylie Jenner posted some photos on Instagram and you saved those photos. You may decide to post 2 photos on the first page, then use Next or numbered navigation to send your readers to other pages with the rest of the pictures.

This approach could double and even triple the page views on your content, reduce bounce rates and have a positive impact in your bank account.

65. Implement caching when traffic begins to increase

"Clear Cache" is a popular phrase yet many haven't cared to find out the meaning of cache. Cache can exist in several forms. In your browser, it could just be temporal files saved from web pages to save you some data and time when next your browser visits that specific web page again. Several images we see on certain websites are loaded from cache, rather than re-downloading the images again.

In the case of your blog, there are scripts that run on the server, interacting with databases and processing some functions to produce a web page. This can happen each time a visitor comes to your website. When the amount of running processes become excessive or gets over a certain limit, a website can crash or show a 500 Internal Server Error. A cache can be a saved version of a processed webpage on the server that is served to the browser when it requests for the content. This means that the webpage is generated once and saved, saving the server some computing resources.

But the issue with cache is that if you don't set an expiry, it can keep showing old content even when you have updated the content of the page. If you use Wordpress, there are many cache plugins that will help. When you update the content of the page, you should also remember to clear or purge cache on your website. Blogger.com won't have this issue because Google already has a robust server on which the scripts run on.

66. Let Twitterfeed and Hootsuite help

Visit Twitterfeed.com or Hootsuite.com after reading this.

I have tried to manage many social media accounts and that could be a very herculean job. There are free automated softwares that can help you run those. Twitterfeed is one of them and they are in no way affiliated with Twitter.

With Twitterfeed, you can automatically publish posts via feeds to many Facebook pages, timeline, Twitter account, Linkedin profile etc. Twitterfeed will check an RSS feed which is present in most Wordpress sites, and when there is an update, it publishes that update to the connected services like a Twitter account. It is a very nice tool and yet free.

Hootsuite is much more complex platform that can be used to manage many social media accounts at once. With Hootsuite, you can also post to a Facebook Group without going on Facebook.

These tools will reduce the stress of blogging by almost 30%. But when you do have the time, visit the social media websites to know the latest changes and updates made.

If you keep using the third party applications without visiting the social media platforms directly, you may have issues coping with the social media platform when major changes happen or when the third party goes out of service. And it seems Twitterfeed has gone out of service. But there are several alternatives.

67. AdWords could be good for business

Have you ever searched for something on Google only to find some search results with "Ads" inscription? These are sponsored content. People pay for their advertisements to be shown on Google search results.

Is there a word or phrase you would like your website address to rank very high in when people search for them? That can be done through the Google Adwords program, and it is not free.

Assuming you want your blog to be shown when someone types "Lifestyle blogger in New York", all you need to do is target that keyword through Adwords and place a budget. You can set the maximum amount you are willing to pay or let Google do that for you automatically, but note that rates could go high sometimes and you might end up exhausting your daily budget in one click that would be useless. Other times, you might pay a cent for a single click that will change your life. You never know might be searching for a lifestyle blogger in your area. It could be a new company that has a fat budget to give you anything to post something for them, or government hoping to push an agenda through your blog.

Google Adwords program is good for some businesses, especially when people search for the words linked to those businesses on Google all the time. Please note that Adwords is not the only way to appear on Google search results; there are organic methods which we shall treat later.

68. Submit to Google news

Google News at news.google.com has become one of the best news feed. Some people end up there because it curates news from various sources and groups them according to categories and locations. If your blog is not on Google News, then you are probably missing out on the huge traffic hub.

Even when you search for some breaking news on Google, the blogs that exist on the Google News platform tend to appear on top. But submitting to Google news is not an easy process.

If you are a lone blogger, then maybe this isn't for you. If you copy people's content, Google news may not be for you. The same applies to blogs whose content aren't exactly news on their niches. If you write about web development in your blog, and that's what the blog is all about, you are not eligible.

Only few will find it helpful, but the requirements are huge. You need to have a dedicated page where all the editors or journalists are listed. You also need to have a privacy policy, contact page with full address and phone, and then of course categorize your content. We will talk about content categories later on.

Google's Accelerated Mobile Pages Project AMP is another programme that can help you get to Google news faster. There are AMP plugins for Wordpress.

69. Use BBM channel for sure traffic

It would still be early if you jump on this platform right now. A BBM Channel with about 40,000 subscribers is far much better than a Facebook page with 100,000 fans. I know what I am saying unless Facebook decides to change its algorithm on how posts reach the fans. On BBM channels, reach could be over 50%, depending on when the subscribers visit the feed.

Download the latest Blackberry Messenger App and enjoy all the features of the BBM Channel. There is also a web App that can help you manage your channel from a web browser.

You can even promote your BBM channel with Blackberry officially, but you must have a very high budget to do that.

BBM channels convert well in the form of traffic, but monitoring this traffic is an issue. I will show you how to monitor the traffic in the next section.

UPDATE: BBM Channel seemed to have dropped in popularity since 2016 when the first edition of this book was written.

70. Monitor BBM Channel Ads with URL shortening services

When you want to advertise on a BBM Channel, you are required to craft a title for the post, add a photo, then a little description alongside link to the post.

Since you have limited space to write on, there is need to shorten the url. Use goo.gl to shorten urls. The goo.gl link will also monitor the number of clicks on that link, alongside several other data.

But on the Google analytics platform, traffic from BBM Channel will show up as unkown. You can decide to create a new source through the url before you shorten it by adding this:

```
utm_source=BBM&utm_medium=BBM&utm_campaign=BBM
```

Assuming the url was: myblog.com/

Make the new url
myblog.com/?utm_source=BBM&utm_medium=BBM&utm_campaign=BBM

Using the Google Analytics tool, you will notice that a source with name BBM has appeared in the data.

You can use this method to track traffic across multiple channels too, not just on BBM. Remember, since doing this will make the url very long, always shorten with goo.gl

71. Use Facebook groups and girl profiles to drive traffic

I shouldn't be advising you to do this, but it is better than trying to spam people. There are other ways to drive traffic without hacking into people's account. Many hack other people's account on Facebook and post raunchy stuff. That's a crime!

There are a lot of men on Facebook that will like anything that comes from a female profile. If you are a pretty female, count yourself lucky. If not, find a very pretty photo and use it to create a Facebook account. Please don't use this account for anything else other than driving traffic to a legitimate blog.

Add few people as friends and you will find lots of men, and even women, sending you friend requests. As long as you keep accepting, it wouldn't take a week to get to 5000 friends. Others will follow you (they won't be friends with you but can see what you post publicly on their timeline.) This could give you access to about 1000 page views a day. Some create several profiles and use Twitterfeed to post to them all at once. This is a blackhat method of driving traffic.

Anything else you do with the Facebook account is at your own risk, as Police could arrest you for impersonating.

As for Facebook group, just create a group and add people. The surest way to add is through a pretty female profile. Most men tend to be calm when this happens. But women might start asking questions. Do not post too often on the group. Twice a day is OK, until it grows to around 100,000 members.

72. Experiment ad layouts and rotate ads

Now that you have seen how to drive traffic without spending money, you may want to see how the traffic you drive affects your earnings.

First, all your Google Adsense Ads at every position must be from a different Ad units. This will help you track which Ad is making you the most money. You may also decide to switch from responsive to 300X250 ads. Make sure you record the date of this change.

After some days, compare the data from when the Ad was responsive and when the block Ad was replaced and see which has the better CTR and CPC. In fact, what justifies is the final earnings.

Over a specific number of days, an Ad unit with a CPC of $0.08 might have a CTR of 1% and makes you $10 while another Ad unit with a CPC of $0.1 and a CTR of 0.8% makes $15. Even with lower CTR, I might decide to go with the latter. But remember that the reason for the rotation and changing of Ad layout was to increase CTR. From the goals of the experiment, the Ad with higher CTR but lower earnings should be chosen.

CPC might change based on user interest or on page content. So, with better CTR optimization, earnings could triple.

Also take note of new Google Adsense Ad Units which you must use. They are called Page-level ads which once added to the header of your webpage, the ads will come in naturally in any space they deem fit.

You can also use Experiments which is available in Google Adsense Lab from your dashboard. These tools will make your work easier and faster.

73. Consider a redesign every few years, unless you are on Blogger

There are many reasons why the Coca-Cola bottle has changed over time. It's not because science suggested the newer bottles to be better than the older ones. It's simply because they know people get tired of something they have gotten used to over time.

A redesigned blog sparks up interest, even without a new feature. Goal.com does that and it has always been a huge success. There are also advantages to re-designing since better technologies are developed every day. But besides implementing the latest technologies, no blog should look the same way after about 3 years. That doesn't make sense.

The only bloggers who can be excused from this redesign are those locked in the world of Blogger. It seems technology is leaving them behind, and don't be surprised if Google develops a new solution to make Blogger match up with Wordpress.

For Wordpress users, a redesign is as simple as purchasing a new theme and installing. Some themes might require customization though. Remember to keep a backup before doing this.

74. You Must Know SEO

SEO simply means search engine optimization. With a good knowledge of SEO, search engines (like Google, Yahoo, Yandex, Bing etc.) will put a link to your website up for people searching with related keywords. For almost any important keyword, there are thousands to millions of other websites that compete to rank on the first page of popular search engines.

Why should your own content be shown first? Were you the first to write about that keyword, or would you be the last? You simply have no claim to a first page unless you do your SEO well.

Your title must be filled with the most important keyword in the content. If you are writing about how leather bags are produced in Kenya, make sure the keywords "leather, bag, Kenya" are mentioned in your title. In fact, you may decide to use what someone will likely search on Google. Example could be:

> "Where to find leather bag manufacturers in Kenya."

With a good work on the title, make sure they are nested within a <h1> tag. Here comes HTML again. Most themes would do this for you automatically. Any other sub heading must be in <h2> tags as too many <h1> on the same page could cause confusion about what the true title is for the search engine robot.

Even when writing, use other related words and make them bold. For example, you can write:

> Have you been wondering where to find **leather bags in Kenya**? Your search is over. Factory A is a **leather bag manufacturer in Kenya** and they are the best.

That's the secret of SEO. Then make sure Google crawls your content through the Google Webmaster tool. You can fetch any page as Google and then submit it to index. Your content could be on Google search just a few minutes after writing it with these steps.

Also remember to exchange posts with other bloggers so that your link would appear on other websites. Your link on other websites, also called backlinks, are also going to improve your performance on search engines.

75. Use Google for your default site search

If there is no argument about who the best search engine is. Why do you think you can provide the best search for your blog? The traditional search widget on Wordpress is good, but not good enough. If you have been following, then there are just few things you will need to do to make your blog search as sharp as Google.

Remember to make sure Google crawls your content as soon as they are created. You can equally do that yourself. If you were accepted into the Adsense program, there is a tool called Adsense for Search. The search code will show a search box on your website that will work just like the traditional Google search we all know, only that the content shown will only come from your blog.

You can equally earn from Google when people click on adverts that come with the search results.

If however you have not been accepted into the Adsense program, you can still leverage in the power of Google search for your site. Make sure Google crawls your site frequently or try and fetch new content as Google, then submit to index through the Google webmaster tool. You may need a bit programming to achieve this though.

When someone performs a search, capture the search keyword and attach your blog domain name to it to indicate you want Google to search only through your site. Then redirect the person to Google search page. This is how:

> If someone searches for "Kim Kardashian", change the search keyword to "site:myblog.com Kim Kardashian", then url encode the keyword with php.
>
> $keyword= "site:myblog.com Kim Kardashian";
>
> $key=Urlencode($keyword);
>
> Then redirect to this link: https://www.google.com/search?q=$key

I apologize for any inconvenience this may have caused you. Please look for a PHP developer to help you out with this.

76. Ignore earnings sometimes and just post

As an Adsense blogger, you will be inclined to check your earnings several times a day, getting motivated when you are close to your target, and getting depressed when you are unable to reach your target. When earnings are low, this may likely affect post quality. Although for some others, it might become a motivation factor.

There are others who simply stop writing when they have reached their earning targets. After all, planet earth is blue and there is nothing left to do. Indeed, there are characters in this world.

If as a blogger you can learn to ignore earnings and just work, you may notice that your passion would no longer be driven by earnings. The result is an ever-improving quality in posts irrespective of what's happening in the bank.

Bloggers often forget that they aren't writing for Adsense but human beings, and should only be worried when people don't respond to their content. The only time you should really get worried is when people fail to consume your content. As long as the traffic keeps coming and increasing, you have great potential to monetize your content in the future. Remember that content is king and traffic queen.

Stop looking at RPM (Revenue Per Mille) while others are busy creating good content.

77. Ask for or accept content for free from your popular readers

You can do some charity for your fans some times, especially during events that mean so much to them. You can publish their birthday party pictures, wedding pictures or anniversaries. This will create a bond between you as a blogger and the readers. They will likely never forget your blog when you do this.

You can also request for pictures yourself from people for contest or challenge. For example, you may decide to put all the pictures in a post and number them, and then ask the fans to guess a name for each person. The reader with the highest correct guesses wins.

The content you accept could also be event witnessed by a popular reader of your blog. And remember to say that a fan sent it in while posting. That's how some bloggers are able to publish fresh and original materials even when they live miles away from where an event occurred.

Just let your readers know that they can actually send in events happening around them for you. CNN has this ireporter where they do this same thing.

78. Develop a good typing skill to save time

Do you know that a good typing skill can save half a day for you, half a week and half a year, and in fact give you more time to relax and rest for the sake of your health? If you doubt the benefit of good typing skill, take a trip to a popular business centre where students prepare project materials. Compare the amount of money fast typists make with what slow typists make.

If you have poor typing skills, you may spend 30 minutes preparing and formatting a post while another blogger spends just 7 minutes to do the same. The result is that a breaking news you discovered before a fast typist will be published on the fast typist's website before you get your own ready. The fast typist will enjoy more spare times, and will get a *crown* as the first to have broken the news.

You must not go to a computer school to learn to type fast; softwares like the Mavis Beacon will be there to guide you.

79. Avoid over-sharing on your personal Facebook Timeline

Sometimes the way some people share links to their blog posts on their personal Facebook timeline make me believe they are either fake profiles or their account have been hacked. When you share too many blog posts on your Facebook timeline, some of your friends will learn to ignore you, even when you post something important. Some will even find a way to silently unfriend or unfollow you. Yes, some friends are that *unfaithful,* if that's what you have chosen to call them.

If you must share on Facebook, as I have earlier suggested, create a Facebook page or group. Sharing on your timeline should not exceed 3 links to your blog posts per day. And doing that daily is even excessive. You should really avoid it.

While sharing on your personal timeline, remember to only share the most important of posts. If it must be on your timeline, it must have to be worth it.

80. **You should know which page gives you the most money**

Even though earnings shouldn't bother you, but at least once or twice in a day, you should take a look at earnings. One bad thing about Google Adsense is that you don't see the specific pages that make you money. But with good combination of Google Analytics and Google Adsense, you will be able to see that.

Start by linking the Google Analytics Property to your Google Adsense account. When that has happened, give it 24 hours to start showing data. Remember to take a look at the Google Analytics Academy if you have issues doing this.

To see which pages are making you the most money, browse to Behaviour, then Publisher, and then click on Overview. Overview will show you a summary of earnings over the selected period, and then show other data such as RPM, CPC, CTR etc.

Click on Publisher Pages to see how much each page generated. Some pages will keep generating money years after they have been created. Feature posts are good at this. That's why you should do more of that to support your blog when there is no viral story.

You can even see Publisher referrals, to see where those who clicked on your Ads came from.

If you can find how much each page made for you, then you can compare if your promotion of specific content was worth it. If you boost a post for $10 and the post makes you $10, it's bad business. You need profit. You already know how to check if you made profit on the micro level rather than comparing your entire earnings. If you compare the entire earnings to what you spent on a certain day, some parts of the earnings may actually be returns from investments you made years ago.

The last paragraph explained further: When you spend $10 on Facebook boosting of a post and on that same day you make $10 from Adsense, there are possibilities that the $10 spent only made you $5 directly. The remaining earning of $5 may have come from old posts which people are reading and clicking ads on them on that same day. The only way to find out is by monitoring earnings by pages, and not just the entire earnings from the website.

81. If you report news, avoid taking side. If you analyze news, you can condemn or take side

Some bloggers forget the difference between reporting and analysis of an event. While reporting, say what happened and don't give judgment. If a Policeman kicked a woman, say that a policeman kicked a woman. Not that a policeman abused a woman. Leave the judgment to be determined by the reader.

If however you are giving analysis of the event, you may give your own opinion and say it was an abuse and then condemn the policeman. Did you report the circumstances that forced the policeman to kick the woman? That could give further clues.

Don't say that "North Korea is evil" as a state. Rather say what they did that made them evil. Leave the judgment to readers, unless your personal opinion was required.

82. You are in a competition with other bloggers in your niche

Whether you believe it or not, other bloggers in your niche and even those not in your niche would want to conquer you and take over your traffic sources. Most bloggers are ambitious and that's a good thing – that's why you see them attacking about any politician, celebrity, clergy etc. all for the purpose of trending and to drive traffic. It is difficult to find a blogger genuinely interested in helping another blogger, unless there is something in there for him or her.

As a blogger, you really need to be able to carry out research on your own, read about anything you can find about any issue and pay a web designer/developer to come to your aid whenever you need help. Never put all your hopes on another blogger unless he or she is someone you either trust so well or a very close relative/associate.

Do you think CNN would help BBC when they are competing over the same audience? Or you believe YouTube would help Vimeo? You would be wrong to think Yahoo! And Google are in good terms! The same applies to bloggers fighting/competing for audience in the same niche.

83. Get ready to fast and stay awake on a busy day

As a blogger, you may be inspired to write a post as early as 3 AM in the morning. After doing this, you will find yourself writing more until the break of day. You will find yourself browsing across several websites to find news articles to rewrite. You will in fact find yourself writing till midday, and that could even not be the end. It is possible for a blogger to stay put on the computer from early morning till evening, not thinking of what to eat or where to go.

A friend once joked about how people whose partners are bloggers don't need to worry about being cheated on, because serious bloggers don't even have time for themselves, talk more of cheating. Unless a blogger brushes his or her teeth before starting to work for the day, you may find out that the brushing would be postponed indefinitely, till maybe close to mid day or evening.

As a blogger, even if you can afford a lot of luxuries, don't think you will live a luxurious life. Bloggers must be ready to fast. As a blogger, you must be trained to work for several hours without eating.

To help yourself with this lifestyle, always have fast food and junk in the fridge, to avoid developing stomach ulcers and other health complications as a result of constant fasting. But as a blogger, always be ready to fast on a busy day – and most days are going to be busy.

84. When you find a hit post, do more of such and link

One good thing about blogging, especially in the niche of celebrity gossip is that stories develop, linger and spiral into even better stories. Think about Kim Kardashian breaking the internet. It might start as a normal story, but then you will find other celebrities reacting to the news, including the husband. If this kind of story could draw you huge traffic, then a follow up should be able to do more. Make sure they are all linked in such a way that after one is done reading any of the story, you point out a related story like: "See what Kanye has to say about his wife posing naked for Paper Magazine."

One thing you must not do about a hit post is putting all of them on your home page or front page, because it might look like you have nothing else to post about. Imagine coming on your front page and 7 out of 10 articles right there are about a particular celebrity – Bruce Jenner or Caitlyn Jenner. What has this family done to you?

When you link up similar stories, make sure only the hottest is on your homepage. If you do have a sidebar for popular stories, it is cool for those similar stories to take over the top 10 if they are really that popular, but not your home page feed.

When you can't find anything else to post to mix up with the hit stories on a particular celebrity, find a feature post, even if it's from years ago.

85. Avoid sending readers away from your site, unless it makes ene

Your traffic is your money. Several things can make sense, but not everything can make money sense. But one goal you must strive to reach: anytime you send visitors out of your site, it should make you money.

Kylie Jenner just posted a photo on Instagram. You screen grabbed the photo, posted it on your blog and then you put a link back to the original Instagram post asking your readers to check out the original photo there. It doesn't make money sense, unless Kylie Jenner paid you to send traffic to her Instagram photo.

It is good to link to a source of a news article, but mind how you do that and make sure the link opens in a new tab, also known as blank target. Don't make the entire paragraph a link, just where you mentioned the name of the source. Example is: According to CNN, Donald Trump was in New York today to commission... You see how only the CNN is linked. Only the colour shows that. Avoid making links bold, unless you actually want people to click on it. And for you to want them to click on it, it must make money sense.

People can follow you on your social media accounts right from your blog. You don't really need to send them away from your blog and into the social media because once they are done liking or following you, they will head up to see their notifications and they are gone from your website. Therefore, avoid linking to your social media account – use plugins that let them subscribe right from your blog instead.

86. Backup once in a while

Backup is serious and very important. This evens the most important sections – content and traffic. When we talked about Traffic and Content and made them king and queen, ability to retain a backup should be made prince, and then monetization the princess. A blog without a backup is like a business without insurance. You are living in fool's paradise, even if you are on Blogger.

The reason why backup is so important is not just in the event of server failure, it could also be helpful in the event of hack. A hacker can get into a Blogger account and delete everything in there – every single post. I can't give a reason for this, but people are weird.

A server could fail, and the server's backup could also fail. If that happens to your Wordpress blog, what would you fall back to? A plugin or theme or an upgrade is even enough to mess up your database. You really need to backup every month or two.

The things to backup in a Wordpress blog are mostly database and media files. Anything else can be recreated. In the case of blogger, you may just export an XML file that holds your data and a link to your files.

When you backup, you should keep the backup files in a secure place. You can try a separate external hard disk, Drop box or any other file host that is safe. Also, the backup files should be named according to the date they were generated on. Backup gives you insurance and the task of doing it is the premium you have to pay.

If you love the design of your Wordpress website and fear that you might mess it up when you make changes, backup the entire files. This could save you extra cost of getting your web designer to work on your designs again.

87. Get inspirations by getting away from your tools

Blogging requires writing and to write requires one to be creative. There are times when Writer's Block will take over. At times like this, all you need to do is to get away from the tools you use for work such as laptop, phone, writing materials and even television. Just take a walk to the park with nothing. There's nothing as relaxing for a blogger as than taking a walk alone. That's the best way to equip your brain with new things to write about.

Let the breeze revolve around you, let the leaves from the trees rain on you, and the aura of the flowers take your mind away from your immediate world. When your mind is away from your immediate world, then you can think outside your immediate world.

When new things start popping into your mind, ignore them. At this stage, you will feel the urge to rush back and start typing. You don't need to show your brain how desperate you are with those new ideas. Relax and you will see how desperate several ideas in your head will get, competing to be the first to be written about. At this stage, your writer's block will no longer find a reason to be around you – it'll head to the next block.

Take your time. The aim is to let your brain relax. If possible, sleep or just forget about every worry. Get back to your computer after several hours and start jotting down all the new ideas. Elaborate on them later on.

88. Done is better than Perfect

There are times when we want an article to be as brilliant and sharp as something coming out from the mouth of the most inspirational speaker in this world. How do you measure how sharp and brilliant something is? It could be subjective and relative. There's a saying I learnt from someone who has worked at Facebook: "Done is better than Perfect."

A perfect idea that has not been implemented is still of no use. A mediocre idea that has been implemented is better than that perfect idea, until the perfect idea is tested. That's the origin. Programmers can come up with initial versions of scripts that are dirty. But with time, they will brush these scripts up until they become perfect. A writer can also do that.

When you have an idea to write about, start typing at once. When you think it's good to be published, not better or best, publish at once. If you have other ideas about that same article, you can edit and update. That's how you should roll.

89. You can do an eBook when you have much to say, and make money with it

Sometimes you can have an idea that is too much as a blog post. Yes you can divide them into multiple pages or multiple blog post, as series. But you can also compile them all into an ebook, just like the guide you are reading right now. There are a lot of ebook market places on the internet where you can sell the books and make some money.

Amazon.com

Lulu.com

BarnesandNobles.com etc.

Ebook makes reading easier for your site visitors. They can buy the ebook and read offline, whereas they can't read across multiple pages on your blog without saving multiple pages.

Make sure whatever you make an ebook offers value worth more than any single page on the internet. Your ebook should offer a value such that if you decide to make each tip a blog post, up to 20 valuable posts will be made available. And each of the ebook pages will be more useful than any single web-page on that topic.

90. Save title ideas as draft and write later

To avoid forgetting to write about those ideas you have jotted down on papers, sticky note and Write Space, make new ideas post titles and just save as draft. Each time you return to your blog's admin area, you will find them there staring at you, begging to be completed and published.

This will even make collaboration across many devices easier for you. For example, the title you create from an iPhone while in a bus/train can be expanded from your Android tablet while waiting for someone at a reception, and even expanded more when you get home and jump on a computer.

Every opportunity you get to grab an idea, make it a post title and just save as draft. This will make your blog a very fertile land full of ideas.

91. Don't limit yourself to a single blog when you have other ideas

Managing a single blog and dedicating all your efforts to it is a good thing, but not when you have other ideas outside your immediate niche. You may run a blog on health because you went to medical school and be successful with that blog. But you watch football a lot, and you know a lot about that game. Don't let your profession limit you to what you can write about. Create a new blog on sports or football and start off – you may even find football more interesting than the health you've been writing about.

There are people who are into automobile blogging, and have really been following celebrity gossip. Did anyone place a limit on your reach? Get into other things you can blog about, but create a different blog if the niche is entirely different.

There are people who in a bid to increase their income from blogging create different other blogs in the same niche containing the same exact content with their first blog. The only implication is that you may end up dividing the audience you already have and even reduce how search engines rank your blogs. What you can do is hire someone to take care of the other blogs, so the contents can vary.

92. Don't tell readers what you earn

Among your readers are those looking for an opportunity to devour/exploit you – believe it or not.

One thing you should avoid doing is revealing how much you make every month to your readers. Apart from the security implications on your life and in your business, you may just end up making readers hate your personality.

It is enough to say that the month has been good, or that the year has been good, but not that you made $7,500 this month with Adsense. Some will take you as a show-off. Celebrities do that a lot though.

Adsense, according to their policy, even prohibits bloggers from publishing details of their earnings. You may end up losing your Adsense account if you do this.

As per security, you never know who knows where you live and where you bank and who can get access to your banking details, depending on how security conscious you are. But if you are security conscious, then you shouldn't be the guy or babe posting how much he or she earns on the internet. You can end up making yourself a victim of theft. Worse is that you attracted the thieves.

93. Use pidgin but avoid swear no matter what

Every blogger came from somewhere. Depending on how connected you are to a specific country or city, you may use pidgin to connect more with your audience. Pidgin can boost originality by giving you a voice.

Also know when to use pidgin. If your topic is mostly on professional matters like serious issues, giving health advice, banking and finance, I don't see how much pidgin will help. But on politics and celebrity, pidgin will surely be good.

While you are free to use pidgin, there are words you must try your best to avoid. Even censoring would not help with these two words. The two words you must avoid at all cost are:

| Fuck |
| Shit |

They should never come close to your vocabulary. Don't even think of censoring them.

94. Censor words to avoid being flagged automatically

There are other words you may wish to use, but unless you are a health blogger, try and censor them as follows:

Penis turns to P3n!s or P*nis or even Joystick

If I have shown you this, then you probably know what to do with others. This will help save you even from robots that raise red flags automatically from words detected on web pages.

This will save your @$$ from getting flagged by Google search.

95. Program yourself to post with mobile at busy times

You must be a blogger everywhere you go, and it is by taking advantage of the power of mobile devices that you can achieve that. We have gotten to the age where computing power of mobile devices can match the computers. You should learn to take advantage of some dedicated software for blogging with a mobile device.

Wordpress users can actually update their blog through a mobile using a browser, but there is a dedicated Android Application meant for Wordpress which they can use too. This Android Application for Wordpress could offer better computing power on mobile device, at least better than the mobile web browser interface.

Blogger also has a dedicated Android application that can be taken advantage of by Blogger.com users. This also offers better solution more than the web browser interface on mobile devices.

It is understandable if you cannot write a lengthy post via a mobile device. If you ever want to write a lengthy post, then you should use a computer. One major goal of using mobile devices to blog is to catch up with breaking news and break them too. As soon as CNN breaks a news, and you read that while in a bus/train, you can quickly do a short post on that news with a mobile device too. Remember to attach "More details later" and of course "according to CNN" if that news came from CNN.

96. Take off Pop up Ads if you love your audience

Pop up Ads can be very annoying and a lot of blogs use this to chase potential fans away. Pop up ads coming up when the visitor has reached a certain part of the page won't be that bad, but the one that comes up each time a page is opened is as bad as using a mega phone to draw the attention of a customer sleeping in your reception.

Pop up ads are even a red flag according to Adsense policy. Most bloggers use Adsense and if you read through their Dos and Don'ts, you will find a limitation to the use of Pop ups.

If you need to draw attention, try keeping the content of a pop up just above the fold, in a dark background, and then make sure the height of the box is big enough that the reader does not see any part of the page's content. But let the reader know that he or she can scroll down to read the content of the page. At least, this won't come as a surprise to the visitor and there will be no need to click on anything to close the pop up.

Another solution is to do this exact thing, but place the box just below the content.

97. Know in detail who most of your readers are

You can actually track a lot of data about your audience if you want to. The tool is in Google Analytics. Knowing some details about your audience can help with what they need. Using Google Analytics Audience Overview can show you the country of residence and city, and even Telecommunication networks most of your readers use.

You can see the screen size of majority of your visitors. Think about what you can achieve with this data. Assuming most of your visitors record a screen width larger than 800 pixels, it means that most of them visit with tablets and computers. Advertising programs that run on computers could be a good business. But when data show that majority use screen less than 500 pixels in width, then majority use mobile, and advertising mobile products would be good business.

Country can also be important when deciding what to promote to them and what language to use. Assuming majority of your visitors are from India but you have been posting about celebrities in the UK, what does this tell you? It is possible they are genuinely interested in UK celebrities, but you can mix this up with Indian celebrities and it would make sense.

You can even use Facebook Insights to know about fans on your Facebook page. You can see their age-range, gender and countries. Never ignore the importance of monitoring your data. But please remember the GDPR and do let them know the data you collect, how you use them and for how long you retain them.

98. Expect to get SEO requests from Indian Based Web Companies

In case you start getting lots of requests about how your blog could be made to stay on the first page of Google for specific keywords in your niche, don't ever get startled up that maybe something is not right about your blog and now people are seeing it. Indian web based SEO companies, as they call themselves, send a lot of Spam emails to websites and blog owners daily, marketing SEO with lots of promises.

If you really need that, you can pay them to deliver their services, but don't think it's a big deal. The SEO tips I already taught you are what they will still do for you, except this time they may include backlinks which could raise a red flag from search engine depending on how it was used.

But even after you have used the services of a company for SEO, other companies will keep sending you emails. And even the company that just delivered a service to you might still send you a spam email to get their services again.

When you start getting lots of those emails, simply send them to the spam folder or delete, unless you do need the services. But you will get lots of emails, as long as your email is on the contact page.

99. Categorize Content unless your Niche isn't vast

You need to sort your content according to sub categories in your niche. Even in football, you will find some categories like Transfer News, Goals, Premier League, and UEFA Champions League. There is no niche that can't be sub-divided. You will only combine them if you are too lazy to split.

Separating or categorizing your content can attract more readers, and sooner or later, you will start noticing that your fans are in factions. Assuming your blog is about health, you can have male health, female health, etc. If you do this, you will notice specific people commenting and sharing articles and news only on a particular category.

Categorizing shows your ability to keep things in order. Creating categories might be a mind-boggling task since many categories will be needed to make a blog complete, and yet you will find many categories almost similar. The easiest way to solve this problem of having similar categories is to combine those categories into one.

Fashion and Modeling, Food and Nutrition, News and Events etc.

As per having so many categories, your niche will determine the basic ones needed, then you can combine others into a category for everything named General, Odd, All, Others or More.

If you will find it difficult to update several categories, please stick to 2 or 3 categories or drop categories entirely.

100. Invest your money elsewhere in case you get tired

Don't ever think you will be a blogger forever. The passion could die out, or other conditions could make the job unfavorable. Apart from having other things doing, make sure that you channel the money you make from your blog into other sustainable businesses. Contact professionals to help you invest elsewhere.

Don't make luxury acquisition your priority if you happen to be making huge money currently. Make investment your priority. The returns from those investments could then be used to acquire luxuries.

For example, you may decide to build student's hostel close to a new university with money running into millions, then purchase a luxury car with the first rent payments, which could be in thousands, depending on the currency we are counting on. Winks!!!

101. Never Close a Blog; Sell it instead

You find many bloggers closing down blogs for new found love. Why do that when you can leave the money-making machine in the hand of someone else, and even make some cash from it. Even if your blog doesn't make you money, check the domain ranking on Alexa and see if it will be useful to a new blogger.

To sell a blog or domain name, go on sites like

- Afternic.com
- Flippa.com etc.

Additional Information

If after reading and you feel touched, don't fail to drop me an email. You can also request for services mentioned in this book through my business and it shall be fulfilled. The business name is Masterweb Business Solutions Limited. Reach us by email at contact@masterweb.com.ng or visit http://masterweb.com.ng to see what we are up to.

www.ingramcontent.com/pod-product-compliance
Lightning Source LLC
Chambersburg PA
CBHW080932170526
45158CB00008B/2259